LIVING IN THE ARMS OF AN HOURGLASS

A.R. LUCAS

Copyright © 2015 A.R. Lucas
Radiant Sky Publishing Group
All rights reserved.
Edited by Christina Hart
Cover art by Bobby Maccione

ISBN-13: 978-1518617522
ISBN-10: 1518617522

This book is dedicated to anyone I have ever crossed paths with in this life. It is because of these encounters, both good and bad, that I have grown to become who I am today. Through you I have learned much, and because of you I have created something I will forever keep close to my heart. I did not write this for you, my friends. You wrote this for me.

Sometimes
I feel as though I live things
from inside the center
of an hourglass.
There I have a little house,
with little dreams
and little moments
all to myself
as the rest of the world
moves ambitiously outside.
Sometimes I'm okay with it –
the emptiness gives me space
to be inspired.
And sometimes
I wish it were different –
less helpless, more hopeful –
like I could be a part of something
life-changing and huge,
like for once,
time was actually on my side.

I find it
wondrously strange
how yesterdays can
be gone too soon
and tomorrows can
come too early,
yet moments
can last forever.

I learn most things
the hard way –
words never seem to do it
for me.
I don't know why,
but I would rather
take a bullet
and see how it feels,
than listen to someone tell me
how much
it's going to hurt.

I remember when my mother once
told me that all memories –
whether good or bad –
are memories worth remembering.
It wasn't until I grew older
that I fully understood the importance
behind those words.

It is the good memories that help
us believe in something better.

It is the bad memories that help
us become something better.

I had a drink with life a couple nights back
and it may have gotten a little drunk.
It started bragging about how much it likes
to fuck with people and how easy it is
to break them down.

"But aren't people capable of controlling
you if they really wanted to?" I asked.

Life grinned. "They don't know that. Humans
are too consumed by time, as if it were limited."

"And what happens when they figure
it out? Then you'll just be the middle man
to nothing, and time will give up on you."

Life didn't say shit after that.

The funny
thing about time is
it goes by fast,
but it
does
it
slowly.

I am not a blunt man.
I would never tell a woman
she wasn't beautiful,
or tell a child not to believe
in their imagination.
I've been told many times in my life
that a hurtful truth
is still better than a lie,
but I believe some truths
should remain unsaid,
because they not only hurt,
they can destroy.
And my heart is much too big
to watch another human
crumble.

I like watching people –
their movements,
the way they speak,
how they breathe –
it's how I get to know
someone.
And not very often,
but sometimes,
there are seconds when
you can see
a glimpse of their soul –
and I swear
it feels like it's looking
right back at you.

Time moves fast,
too fast.
It seems like just yesterday
I was rushing to grow up,
and now
I'm spending my days
wishing life
would slow down.
I was a kid once –
paying for candy and
falling in mud.
Now I'm a man –
paying the bills and
falling in love.

Who am I?
I ask myself that question
every morning
when I get out of bed.
It's an important question —
more important than
anything else.
Who cares who you were?
Who cares who you're going to be?
Who you are right now —
at this very moment —
that is everything.

Live
every second
like tomorrow
is right now.
You could be
as significant as the sea
and time
still wouldn't
wait for you
to stop wavering.

We all carry burdens.
As time goes on
they grow larger, heavier.
They begin
to weigh you down until
you're so low to the ground
that they become
your only friend.
That moment
is not the end of you.
In fact, it is only the beginning.
Once you decide
to look at things with a
different perspective
and overcome those burdens,
they become weightless.
They become a part of you.
It is then
that you become the very
best version of yourself –
the one who not only survived,
but lived in every shade.

I'm not
as whole as I used to be.
There are pieces of me
in every person
I've ever crossed paths with
and every place
I've ever stepped foot in,
on every road I've taken
and every decision I've made.
This is not necessarily
a bad thing.
I don't consider these pieces "missing."
In their place
rests memories I can look back on,
moments to smile for
and cry for and laugh for.
So I may not be whole,
but that doesn't make me
any less complete.

It's phenomenal
to see how powerful
time can be.
It can turn
a promising child into
a noble leader,
or it could just
as easily turn them
into a monster.

I find myself
questioning things a lot lately –
the people I meet,
the places I go,
the choices I make.
I had always been a "go with the flow"
type of person –
I never bothered to think of the
repercussions or the what ifs –
but times are different now.
I'm older.
I don't trust as easily.
I don't love as easily.
I don't blindly
follow the flow of water,
that I now see
has been tainted
far too many times.

Take your time.
There is nothing wrong
with being particular.
We all want to find someone
who can make the sun
in our hearts
rise a little higher
and burn a little brighter.

There have been
two types of people
in my life –

the ones who
took my heart,

and the ones
who took my heart
for granted.

You, my friend,
are the soil that breathes beneath your feet.
It welcomes your touch,
waits for your warmth
with open arms and a heavy heart,
as does the wind between your hair.
Listen closely and you may hear it chant your name
as if it were a blooming flower's favorite lullaby.

You, my friend,
are the fires that thrive amongst you.
They burn brightly
upon your skin and within your chest,
leaving scorch trails with every step you take.
I have never seen the ground
burn so beautifully, so wild.

And yet somehow you are also
every fiber of the ocean –
calm, a safe haven.
You protect those who do not breathe as you do,
those who do not see as you do.
Hope lies within the deepest shallows of your pupils,
and deeper still, lies sanctuary itself.

I don't know.
It's possible that I just get
attached to things too easily,
or that I like to look back
with no thought
of stepping forward.
Maybe I'm over-thinking this,
but my yesterdays
never seem ready to let me go
when my tomorrows
come knocking to take me
away.

Meet people.
Introduce them
to the deepest parts of you –
all the pretty things
you dream of at night,
what you hope for in the future,
what you have learned from your past.
You wouldn't believe
how beautiful
you could be in the eyes
of someone else.

"I was a lot like you, you know."

"Oh yeah? You went through hell too?"

"Yes," the man said with a smile.
"And I survived, just like you will."

Sometimes I feel as though
I've lost who I used to be.
Although
I guess even the wind changes,
as do the seasons in a year
or the currents of the shore.
Maybe it's human nature
to change along with it.
I'm a completely
different person now,
but why would that make me
any less me?

I can't tell you how many times
my heart and my brain
have gone to war.
They fight and fight and fight
because somehow,
they both know what is best
for me.

"Take the world!"
my brain says.

"Don't take it,"
my heart argues.
"Just love it."

I'm still trying to find the man
in me my mother told me about
when I was a child –
the one who would save the world,
the one who would make
the perfect husband and father.
I've seen him before.
Every now and then
he will do something to remind me
that he exists.
I can only hope that one day
he will be permanent.
After all, beauty can only remain
hidden for so long –
eventually
someone will recognize it.

That's the thing
about time –
there isn't a wound
it can't heal,
a disaster
it can't vanquish,
a city
it can't build,
or a love
it can't grow.

A spark can start
a forest fire.
A kiss can signify
a lifelong marriage.
A choice can destroy
a friendship.
A bite of food can nourish
a hungry child.
An idea can build
an empire.

Don't take
the little things
for granted.

Every day is a new day –
with new opportunities to face
and take advantage of.
Maybe you have a routine –
breakfast and work and dinner and bed.
Pay attention as you
go about the mundane.
There is always
something new amidst the old.
Every day –
no matter where you go
or who you know –
you have opportunities
to create a better life
for yourself or for someone else.
Take them.
You'll be better for it.
You'll feel better for it.
You'll live better because of it.

I miss a lot of things in my life,
and I hate the pain
that comes with the helplessness -
the desperate longing
to satisfy
what the human memory craves.
It hurts, but I think
that is what time intended.
We feel this sense of loss
so we can learn to appreciate
it more when the things we love
fall back into our lives.
If only we could learn to care
for what we have –
not for what we fear of losing –
maybe
we'd stop living with regret
so damn much.

They say life is what we make it
and in most cases it's true,
but there are so many things
that happen that
are out of our control.
Yes, we can make our own decisions
and go about our lives
the way we want to,
but it's important
that we leave our expectations
open to new things.
You never know when life
will decide to mix it up,
make it interesting,
and put a nice dent
in your fancy new sports car.

My mind
is like the home of a hoarder.
There's random crap
all over the floor.
There are boxes
built to the ceiling,
and a closet
full of clothes I'll never wear.
It's trying to juggle so much
to the point of insanity.
I've let so many people into my life
that it can be hard
to keep up with everyone.
I just love everything
too much to let any of it go.
I'm a hoarder of moments.

I wasn't born
with a reason to believe in hope.
I had no father around
to show me what it meant to be a good man.
I had a stressed mother
who came home from work late at night,
struggling to keep the fridge full
so me and my sister could have a reasonable
plate of food for dinner.
As I grew older
I got caught in an unhealthy lifestyle,
which consisted of women, alcohol,
meaningless fights, and staying out way too late –
desperate to find that emotional satisfaction
I craved as a child.
It was like the world was betting against me
from the very beginning,
waiting for the day I exploded into nothingness
like a fallen star that could
never shine bright enough to survive.
I was born inhuman,
and it took not feeling human
to truly appreciate the beauty of being one.

A.R. LUCAS

How
beautiful is it
that humans
change
just as
the leaves
do?

"I need to lose weight,"
she said, gazing at her belly in the mirror.
"I'll start going to the gym
and eating better after New Year's."

I laugh to myself.

It seems like nowadays
everyone talks about tomorrow
as if today doesn't exist.

I have a hard time moving on,
as most people do.
It's human nature to bind ourselves
to moments in our lives
that made us smile –
and that is not necessarily
a bad thing.
There is nothing wrong
with cherishing great memories.
It is when you hold onto old things
so tightly that there is no room
for something new
that you deprive yourself
of something that has
the potential to be indisputably
extraordinary.

When I was a boy,
a man told me to keep
my eyes ahead and my hands
in fists against my sides.
Back then
I believed he was preparing
me for the bullies
on the school yard –
but now I know
that clever bastard
was just trying to prepare me
for life.

It is in our nature.
You're going to make mistakes,
that's inevitable –
how you go about learning
from them is everything.
Will you shrug
and deny the fact
that you did anything wrong?
Or will you accept it,
learn from it,
and move on?
There is not a damn thing
wrong with making a mistake,
I promise you.
Even a butterfly
must struggle through
growth to be the best, most
beautiful version of itself.

You can keep me
in this cage
and I'll still long
for freedom.
Just clip my wings
so the hope
stops hurting.

Humans
weren't meant
to fly.
Humans
were meant
to survive
the fall.

Sometimes it's okay
to be selfish.
So many of us give up
on our dreams and ambitions
in spite of someone else's.
We smile at loved ones as we
watch our hopes run
out the door –
and that is tragic.
Every chance you get,
every moment you have alone,
do something you truly love –
whatever it is.
Scream out the window
at the neighbors.
Dance until your heart
explodes.
Sing like the world is watching
and you're the next big thing.
Bring yourself back to that place
in time where you were as a child –
back when every dream
was a possibility.

I've had a fascination
with hourglasses since I was a child.
Every time I had
the opportunity to flip one,
I would.
I look back on those moments
and laugh at how mesmerized I was,
watching the sand
pour to the bottom of the glass.
You could say
it was because I was a kid –
anything can snatch
a little boy's attention, right?
Yeah, well,
I think it had to do with
a little more than that.
I think subconsciously
I understood how incredible it was.
Time was literally moving
just beyond a thin sheet of glass.
And in the eyes of that little boy,
it was magic.
It was a little thing
called time.

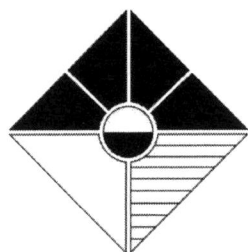